ANDROID PROGRAMMING

For Beginners

The Simple Guide to Learning Android Programming Fast!

Table Of Contents

Contents

Introduction

I want to thank you and congratulate you for downloading the book, "Android Programming For Beginners: The Simple Guide to Learning Android Programming Fast!"

This book contains helpful information about Android programming, what it is, and how to do it. Creating apps can be a fun hobby, and also a profitable venture! Whatever your reasons for wanting to learn Android programming, this book is a great place for you to begin.

You will soon discover the basics of Android app development, and how it differs from IOS and other operating systems. This book includes tips and techniques to help beginners learn the basics of Android programming, and begin developing their own apps!

You will also learn about the different tools, programs, and equipment needed to begin developing Android applications from home.

At the completion of this guide, you will have a good understanding of Android programming, JAVA, how code works, and how to begin developing your very own apps!

Thanks again for downloading this book, I hope you enjoy it!

Chapter 1: This Book and Mobile Operating History

Android is currently the most popular operating system for tablets and smartphones. Aside from Android devices being cheap, Android is more popular than iOS due to the fact that it is not proprietary software — meaning that you can do anything with it.

You can modify your Android OS anytime if you are capable. You can distribute it freely. And virtually, there are no restrictions that you can violate that will result in serious trouble!

This book will introduce you to the basics of programming and the history of mobile applications, companies, and operating systems. In addition, since Android development is mostly based on Java coding, introduction to Java programming is included. However, the book will not go in-depth with Java.

Also, XML will be touched on to make sure that you aren't foreign to the layout files that you might need to edit manually when the time comes. In addition, familiarity with Android Studio will also be discussed just to make sure that you master the main tool in developing Android applications.

Overall, it will prepare you to create and develop apps for Android. Starting from setting up the software development kits and integrated development environments, to creating your very first project and testing it on your device or Android emulator, this book will cover all of these topics.

Roots of Android

Android is made from Linux. Linux is an operating system that is also an open source and has a GPL license (GNU General Public License version 2 to be precise). On the other hand, Linux is based and made from UNIX. As a fun fact, the iOS is made from Mac OS X. And Mac OS X is a UNIX system. Virtually, architecture- and origin-wise, iOS is related to Android.

Android was created by the Open Handset Alliance, which was led by Google. This operating system was built with users and interoperability in mind.

Emergence of Smartphones and Mobile Operating Systems

During the early years of smartphones and smart electronic devices and appliances development, all manufacturers spent a lot of time and money in using and creating operating systems for their products. For example, with smartphones alone, many operating systems were developed. A few of them are LiMo, MeeGo, Maemo, WebOS, Palm OS, Windows Mobile, and Nokia's very own Symbian.

At that time, everything was a mess. Users were always disoriented whenever they changed their phones. In many cases, they tended to let go of their new phones just to go back to their old ones because of the unfamiliarity that a different mobile OS brought to them.

On the other hand, mobile app development was not as robust as it is today. Due to a number of operating systems, creating a program was always a risk. First of all, programmers were limited to creating programs for a small market.

Symbian OS

This slowly changed with Java and Symbian. Because Java programs are interoperable by nature, apps created in Java proliferated. The limitation of operating systems that were created has been relieved a little. Thanks to Java virtual machines, app development for mobile devices and smart appliances flourished.

Aside from that, app development in Symbian was also robust. Multiple programming languages and SDKs were available that allowed app developers to create programs according to their preferences and style. A few of those languages and SDKs are Python, Flash Lite, .NET, Ruby, C, C++, Visual Basic, C#, and Qt.

Symbian, on the other hand, became one of leading operating systems during its time. Due to the popularity of Nokia, Symbian was used by a lot of people. And thankfully, Nokia was not the only one who used Symbian. Mobile phone manufacturers such as Sony Ericsson, Motorola, and Samsung also used this OS in their products. During the years 2000 — 2010, Symbian was the world's Android.

Popularity of the New Mobile Operating Systems

However, new players in the operating system industry appeared — namely Blackberry, Windows Phone, iOS, and Android. Aside from those, new smartphone technologies appeared. Older OSs were not able to keep up.

The popularity of the fresh names in the industry made those operating systems appear defunct. After all, consumerism worked at its best. Just by adding the name of big brands on any device such as Apple, Microsoft, and Google, the masses will think that it will be the best thing in the world. Try asking anybody, "Do you know what Symbian is?" Most of them will answer no — despite those people most likely having had used a Symbian phone at one point in their lives.

Development of Android

Android seemed like it popped up out of nowhere. Well, it did. Development of the Android operating system was kept secret. Development started in 2003 at Android Inc. The original plan was to create an operating system for digital cameras. However, the market for cameras was not quite big enough to make the effort of developing an operating system worth it.

The key people in Android Inc. upped the ante and targeted the mobile phone industry. They aimed to defeat the reigning Symbian and the not so popular but selling Windows Mobile. The development history of Android Inc. was relatively unknown.

But when Google acquired the company, speculations about the project arose. And after two years of operations with Google, the first Android device on the market emerged — the Nexus.

Android did not become popular because it had Google's name on it alone. For one, Android was able to develop solid standards in the mobile phone industry. Along with the standards, the operating itself was open source — unlike Symbian that was completely proprietary.

Being an open source high-end operating system, Android was able to attract the attention of a lot of developers. On the other hand, they kept some of the 'ideas' and features of other smartphone operating systems to prevent users from getting too overwhelmed by the new operating system and for software developers to become accustomed to the operating system quickly. One of the things that made

Android 'friendly' to app developers is its Dalvik Virtual Machine — a Java virtual machine for Android.

Google Play Store

The emergence of the Google Play Store (formerly Android Market, Google Music, and Google eBookstore) has been crucial to its success. The goal of the Google Play Store is to allow app developers to distribute and sell programs in one place.

It is probable that Google was able to learn from the mistake that Apple made with their iOS and developed Google Play. Around 2007, the iOS was only capable of running proprietary software from Apple. Back then, Steve Jobs believed that web apps were enough to provide iOS users of their supply of their much-needed programs.

However, the iOS was immediately "jailbroken" to allow third-party programs to run in iOS. Due to the 'risks' that it has caused for Apple, in the next release of their iOS, the Apple's App Store was included. The App Store allowed third-party developers to sell and distribute their apps in the App Store. Google responded quickly to this "idea" and launched Google Market a few months later. Blackberry followed suit with its App World a year later.

Despite Apple opening their doors to third-party developers, most of them were unhappy with the terms and conditions that the company imposed in the App Store. Due to that, some developers have relied on selling their apps on Cydia — a third-party software distribution app.

Unlike Apple, Google is more lax when it comes to app submissions in Google Play. However, recent issues like prevalence of malware-infested programs have made Google take action. Now, apps submitted to Google's Developer

Console are scanned by Google Bouncer — Google's antivirus and antimalware software for apps. Also, just this year, Google has employed human reviewers to check submissions.

A Friendly Reminder

So what does all of this mean for you?

First, as an aspiring Android app developer, you must now have an idea about the current environment of the industry you are entering. If you are serious about app development and you are learning Android development to earn money, this part is important for you to know.

As of now, you should understand where you stand. Android has become the leading operating system over the past few years. But who knows, after a few years, what happened to Symbian may happen to Android. Now is the time to act!

Is Android app development the right course to take for you?

The most basic apps have already been created. Most leading development companies have already monopolized Google Play. And the saddest fact about this is that most of their apps are free of charge.

As a sole developer, you have rough days ahead of you. As a student or a person aiming to get employed by those companies, strive harder. You have got a lot of competitors. As a hobbyist, you have nothing to lose except for your time, but expect that you will gain a lot. All of you will gain something.

This part is not meant to scare you away, but to inform you. It's not easy to make a hug app that will earn you millions – it is quite rare. However, if that is your goal, it is still definitely possible with the right idea! If you are still sure you want to keep on learning Android, read on and good luck!

Android Features

Around the years 2007 and 2008, the first version of Android appeared on the market. The SDK or Software Development Kit for creating Android apps became available in 2007. Android is, as of this writing, on version 5.1. Right now, Google is working on Lollipop's successor, Android M. Meanwhile the SDK for Android now comes with Android Studio.

A few of the important features that the Android operating system supports are:

- Connections: UMTC, NFC, Wi-Fi, WiMAX, EDGE, CDMA, GSM, LTE, IDEN, EV-DO, and Bluetooth

- Database: SQLite

- Messaging: SMS and MMS

- Media Format: JPEG, GIF, PNG, BMP, OGG Vorbis, WAV, MIDI, MP3, AAC 5.1, AAC, HE-AAC, AMR-WB, MPEG4, AMR, H.263, and H.264

- Browser: HTML5, CSS3, and JavaScript

- Others: Wi-Fi Direct, Android Beam, Widgets, Multiple Languages, Multi Touch, and GCM

Knowing these features is essential for you to take advantage of them in the programs you can create. Remember that older versions of Android do not support a few of the features of newer phones. For example, versions lower than Android Lollipop cannot fully control a smartphones camera. Older versions can only control a few features such as flash, exposure, and ISO values. Some can control shutter speed, but most cannot control aperture.

Android App Development

Creating apps in Android is similar to creating Java programs. To be honest, the language being used in Android is Java with a different flavor and a different virtual machine. Throughout the years, Google has been making a lot of modifications to the Android SDK and its programming language.

By the way, even though Android has its own Java virtual machine called Dalvik, it cannot run regular Java programs created for computers or old mobile phones. You will need a third party program for them to run. They are usually called Java emulators.

Because Java is the base of the Android programming language, this book will provide you with a basic course on Java development. Expect that you will have a steep learning curve, especially if this is your first time creating programs.

On the other hand, creating, testing, and debugging the Android apps that you create is a bit time consuming. To test your apps, you will need an Android emulator (comes with Android Studio) or a smartphone running on developer mode.

Chapter 2: Android's Architecture

Just like any typical computer system, Android devices have abstraction layers. They are hardware, firmware, assembler, kernel, operating system, and applications. In basic Android app development, you will only need to learn and familiarize yourself with the last three: kernel, operating system, and applications.

The last three combined compose the Android operating system. And the Android operating system can be split into five software components. Those components are applications, application framework, Android runtime, libraries, and the Linux kernel.

The Kernel

The heart (and brain) of an operating system is the kernel. In Android, it uses a Linux kernel. As of this writing, Android is using Linux version 2.6. It also contains 100 or more patches to make it capable of running on most mobile devices.

And because Android runs on a Linux kernel, it is as good as a decent computer — not to mention that that is possible because Android devices have much more processing power now.

In the software component layer model, the kernel is on the bottommost part and it supports everything above it. Without the kernel, any software component will be useless.

The primary job of the kernel is to manage the hardware. It lets software and hardware communicate with each other.

Also, it handles the resources of the device. It acts as a traffic manager for the CPU (Central Processing Unit). It also handles the amount of RAM (Random Access Memory) that will be used by the system and its applications.

Despite hardware components being different from device to device, the kernel can still manage them as long as it has the drivers for those components. Aside from the CPU and RAM, the kernel also handles the camera, screen, memory, keypad, speakers, Wi-Fi, battery, etcetera.

Libraries

Next to the kernel is Android's set of libraries. Libraries are reusable components that applications can use in order to perform advanced and menial tasks. These components allow developers to minimize the amount of time they need to use in development since they do not need to recreate the functions that they can and need to use from Android's libraries.

A few of the most important libraries in Android are libc, SSL, SGL, WebKit, FreeType, ES, OpenGL, SQLite, media framework, and surface manager. WebKit will be used an example for you, so you have an idea of what libraries do in an operating system or application.

The WebKit library allows programs to be capable of rendering HTML files and executing JavaScript code. Currently, the default browser in Android makes full use of this library. On the other hand, WebKit becomes a handy tool in case programmers want to insert a browser snippet in their programs. And due to that, they do not need to code a browser of their own.

Runtime

Together with the libraries, the Runtime is on the next layer of software components in Android. Inside the runtime, two essential sets of files reside. The first is the Dalvik Virtual Machine. And the second is the Java core libraries.

Applications use the runtime in order to run in Android. Since most Android programs are written using Java, they need a virtual machine to run in Android. That is where the Dalvik Virtual Machine comes in. It provides an environment that will translate the Android source code into machine code. Once the source codes of the programs are translated, the processor of an Android device can execute them.

Dalvik comes handy because it is designed to be a virtual machine for small computer systems such as smartphones and tablets. It allows applications to consume less processing power and less RAM.

The java core libraries provide most of the functionalities that Java/Android programs need. It helps the Dalvik Virtual Machine to make Java programs run seamlessly.

Just recently, Google launched Android Runtime or ART. It is supposed to replace Dalvik. The new Android Runtime was included in KitKat (Android 4.4). And it completely replaced Dalvik in Lollipop.

Application Framework

Above the libraries and runtime, is the Application Framework layer of Android. The framework provides applications that allow basic usage of the device Android is on. Most of the applications in this framework are written using Java.

A few of the services or applications in the application framework are the notification, location, resource, telephony, package, window, and activity managers. It also includes the view system and content providers.

These frameworks also allow app developers to have better control of devices that run Android. In order to make use of these services, the developers just need to make their applications communicate with the framework.

Applications

This is where you are going to be busy. All the programs that you will create will fall under this software component layer. By default, an Android system has a few applications that come with it (a few others may be included depending on the device manufacturer). A few of those applications are home, phone, browser, and contacts.

Chapter 3: App Development Preparations

Android app development is not a walk in a park, but that doesn't mean that it is impossible. To be honest, a bit of experience in programming would really help you, especially in Java programming. A bit of experience with some SDKs (Software Development Kits) and IDEs (Integrated Development Environment) such as Java SDK, Eclipse, and Visual Studio would really make things easier for you. Familiarity with XML is also a big plus.

Before you start learning and developing Android apps, you must make sure that you have the following:

A Decent Computer

Unfortunately, it is not ideal to use an old computer when creating Android applications. Modern SDKs such as the Android Studio is computer resource intensive. Even with a decent computer (with 2Ghz processor and 4GB RAM), running the Android Studio can be a struggle.

On the other hand, one of the biggest problems with old computers is that it cannot run the Android emulator properly. Android emulators are applications that allow programmers to test their Android apps on their computers. Compared to the Android SDK, these emulators require higher computer specs in order to run normally.

Android Phone or Tablet

However, do not fret. Without using an Android emulator, you can still test your programs. You can do that by plugging in your Android devices to your computer. Thankfully, Android's developer options make it possible to test Android programs easily.

You do not need to create the application package and send it to your phone directly. You do not need to install it either. Android SDKs will do that for you as long as your phone is connected to your computer.

On the other hand, please make sure that the Android device that you use is the target device for your applications. Take note, testing on a device with a higher Android version may become problematic if you are trying to distribute your app to people with devices that run on lower Android versions. Also, if your target device are tablets, then use a tablet to test your apps.

The SDK

The SDK is the important core in developing Android. All of the writing, designing, and conceptualizing you will do for your future app will happen in here. So what is an SDK anyway?

SDK or Software Development Kit is a set of programs or just a sole program that is made for program development for a certain system or language. These sets of applications' goal is to make everything needed for program development available such as profilers, debuggers, libraries, compilers, etcetera.

In developing programs for Android, the main SDK that you will use is Android Studio, which was created by Google.

Android Studio is an IDE that comes with the Android SDK. You can download it from http://developer.android.com/sdk/index.html. The installation package of the SDK is around 300MB to 400MB.

Despite the 'relatively' small size of the installation file, it will require more than 450MB of your disk space. Not to mention that it will need to download more files from the internet. Due to that, make sure that you have enough free disk space ready.

Android Studio can be installed on Linux distros (that have glibc 2.11), Mac OS X (10.8.5 and later versions), and Windows XP (and later versions). In Linux and Mac OS X, unpack the Android Studio package. On Windows operating systems, just follow the installation wizard.

After installing or unpacking, open the SDK Manager. The SDK Manager will download all of the necessary files. You can select the repositories that you want, but do not do anything yet. By the way, the file sizes of the repositories are huge.

The first update that you perform in the SDK Manager will require you to have 1GB of free space or more. In the case that you are going to use an internet connection with a limited data plan, it is better to download the repositories using a regular internet connection instead.

ADT (Android Development Tools) and Eclipse

Before Android Studio was created, Android developers relied on Eclipse and ADT. Most developers have chosen Eclipse because it is excellent when it comes to Java software development. Since Android programming makes use of Java, Eclipse has become the preferred IDE (Integrated Development Environment).

An Integrated Development Environment is an application that makes it easier for programmers to create programs. An IDE's is to make development easier and faster (and friendlier, too).

On the other hand, ADT or Android Development Tools was a plugin for Eclipse. This plugin enables the IDE to customize Eclipse to be ready for Android programming. For new Android programmers, Eclipse and ADT are good alternatives for Android Studio.

However, it is much better to use Android Studio instead since it is much more robust and updated. Although, the big drawback in Android Studio is that it is slow and a bit bloated.

But if you plan to choose Eclipse, you can download it from http://www.eclipse.org/mobile. The installation file for Eclipse is around 300 to 400MB, Take note that you need to get the latest version of Eclipse to make sure that you will not have problems with creating Android programs. If you have an older version of Eclipse, take note that it must be higher than Eclipse Indigo or version 3.7.2.

JDK (Java Development Kit) and JRE (Java Runtime Environment)

Since Android programming heavily relies on Java, it is essential that your computer has the latest version of Java Runtime Environment. Android Studio and Eclipse depend on Java in order to run and allow you to create Android programs.

With computers running Microsoft Windows, JRE is usually installed. However, make sure that your Java Runtime Environment is fully updated. To update your runtime environment, go to your computer's control panel and look for the Java icon. Open it, and go to the Update tab. Click on the Update Now button to initialize the update. Do note that the update requires an internet connection.

JDK is the development kit for creating Java programs. This kit, on the other hand, does not come preinstalled on your computer. Getting it requires you to visit Oracle's website. The address of the page where you can download the Java Development Kit is http://www.oracle.com/technetwork/java/javase/downloads/index.html. Downloading the JDK might require you to have 1GB of free space in your hard drive ready.

Android Studio

The main reason developers are now shifting to Android Studio is due to its robustness. In Android Studio, you will be able to take advantage of new Google APIs, Android Lollipop platform, Android SDK tools, Android Studio IDE, Live preview, Maven, JUnit, Google Cloud, and Gradle.

Android Studio is the current IDE that Google supports in Android development. Of course, it is theirs after all. Due to that, support for Eclipse has been retired. Aside from the additional plugins, tools, and features, Android Studio has a superb code editor for Android programming. Some of its features are keyword completion, refactoring, and code analysis.

As mentioned before, Android Studio's main drawback is its slowness. You will need to have a computer with decent specs to have a decent programming experience with it. In addition to the Android SDK, the installation file for Android Studio is more than 800MB. Once installed, expect that it will use up 3GB of disk space. Optional packages of Android Studio may require another GB.

Chapter 4: Programming: Java and XML

IDEs have made programming a lot easier, especially when it comes to creating GUIs (Graphical User Interface). Graphical user interface is the graphics that you fiddle with when you use an app. For example, the program that you see when you open up Notepad is Notepad's graphical user interface.

Thanks to Android Studio and Eclipse, you do not need to hard code the contents of your GUIs. All you need to do is to drag and drop the elements that you want to appear in your app. For example, if you want a textbox in your app, you can just drag and drop a textbox widget on the Live Preview of your app (this will be discussed later).

Unfortunately, programming a functional and feature rich app does not only involve designing and dragging and dropping elements on your graphical user interface. You will be forced to write code. Even if you have a textbox in your app, what will you do with the input that the user will type on that? You need to write some code in order to manipulate that data and put it to use.

If you have no idea how to write code, then you will not be able to get far in Android app development. This book will provide you the basics of computer programming. In addition, you will be given a brief course in Java and XML.

Java is a programming language while XML is a markup language. Java programs or files end with the Java file extension. Some other Java files have different file extensions, and you will learn about them later.

On the other hand, XML files end with the .xml file extension. XML is mostly used on the web while some use it in their programs. Android heavily uses XML files in its apps. Take note that both have big roles in Android app development.

Most of your program's functions will be written on Java. Manipulating, storing, changing, and putting your whole program together requires code written on Java. Alternatively, XML files store the settings of your graphical user interface or activities. It has other uses, too, but they will be discussed later.

Introduction to Java Programming

The level of your expertise in Java determines how far you can go in Android development. But do not worry, you do not need to be a master of Java programming in order to create a decent app. As long as you nail down the basics, you will be able to create almost anything that you want.

First and foremost, it is crucial that you understand Java's syntax. Syntax is like grammar rules in English. These rules must be strictly followed. But despite that, these rules are relatively simple and easy to memorize.

The syntax must be strictly followed because if it's not, the computer or your device won't be capable of understanding context. Those machines need clear, concise, and simple instructions. Just one small mistake in your source code and your computer might return an error or might do something else, which you have not planned or intended it to do.

But before you learn the rules of the language, you must know the parts of its regular sentences.

Source Code

Source code is a file that contains computer instructions written in a certain programming language. It is the rawest form of your program and it is probably the most readable and understandable as well. However, the computer cannot understand it.

To make it a runnable program, it must be compiled and translated to machine language. In that state, it will be readable by the computer, but you will not be able to read it. That is how programming works.

In most programming languages, your source code will be mostly written in one file only. However, some might need you to write in two files or more. In Android and Java, your source code will be distributed in multiple files. Even if your program is as simple as saying Hello World to the user, your program will still contain multiple files.

The book will later discuss the different files wherein your source code for your future Android program will be split.

Physical and Logical Lines and Statements

A statement is similar to a sentence in the English language. A sentence delivers a complete thought while a statement delivers a complete and valid command. A sentence has a noun and verb. A statement has variables and operators. To write a proper sentence, a writer must follow grammar rules. To write a proper statement, a programmer must follow syntax.

To end a sentence, you must place a period. To end a statement, you must place a semicolon (;) or statement terminator. If you forget to do that, your program will halt and you will receive a syntax error.

A statement can be called a logical line. Technically, it does not matter how many lines of code a statement might span. As long as it is valid and correct, it is a logical line.

On the other hand, a line of code in your source code is called a physical line. In source code editors, every line is numbered. Take note that a physical line is not always considered a logical line.

Identifiers

Identifiers are like pronouns and nouns in programming languages. They are a combination of letters, numbers, and underscores. And they are used to name certain elements in the program — just like a noun. Also, they can be used as references or pointers — just like a pronoun.

A few of the things that require identifiers or names are variables, functions, and objects. Most user or programmer defined variables, functions, and objects must be named using an identifier. Identifiers make it easy for you to recall, invoke, and remember those elements.

For example:

int x = 123;

In the statement above, a variable was created and named with the identifier x. In case that you will need the variable that stores the integer 123, you will need to use x. For example:

Log.v(TAG, x);

With that statement, the variable x will be used. Its value, which is 123, will be printed or displayed on the log console.

Creating identifiers has some syntax rules. One of them is that identifiers are case sensitive (Java is a case sensitive language). A variable with the identifier 'example' is different from a variable with the identifier 'EXAMPLE'.

Also, identifiers must not start with a number. An identifier can contain one or more characters. A lone underscore is a valid identifier. And just to make it clear, identifiers must not contain symbols except for the underscore.

Identifier Naming Convention

Different developers have different naming conventions for their identifiers. During the old times, most developers started their variables with underscores, especially if they were naming a function. On the other hand, some just stick with lower case and simply name their variables with whatever they come up with.

In case that developers want to create a variable with two or more words to make the identifier easy to remember, they use an underscore to separate the words. For example: this_is_an_example_variable.

On the other hand, most Java programmers prefer to use CamelCase on their variables. That is done by capitalizing the first letter of every word in the identifier. Usually, the first letter of the identifier is left in lower case. For example: thisIsAnExampleVariable.

It is much preferred to use CamelCase when programming Java or Android. After all, most keywords and functions in Java are written that way.

Keywords

Keywords are reserved identifiers. They are assigned to built-in functions, variables, and objects in a programming language. Since theses identifiers are already used, you cannot use them anymore. If you do, your program will return an error.

When using a source code editor when writing your program, it is usual that keywords are highlighted in blue and use bold font. This makes it easier for you to distinguish them. Java has more than 50 keywords. In Android, there are a lot.

A few of the keywords you will use a lot in Android or Java programming are: if, or, and, return, public, static, void, and import.

Literals

When creating a program, you will need to input some data that you will need to manipulate and set. Those data can be in form of numbers and text. In programming, numbers are called numerical literals and texts are called string literals.

Numbers can be inputted as is in your source code. For example:

int x = 123;

In the example, it is understood that you want to store the numerical literal 123 in variable x. Alternatively, you can present or input your numerical in different forms such as decimal, hexadecimal, octal, and binary.

However, if you want to store or use text in your program, you will need to enclose the text inside single or double quotation marks. If you do not, the compiler or the IDE/SDK will be confused. The compiler might treat your strings as identifiers or keywords. And in case that the compiler realizes that the text is not a keyword or an identifier for some element, it will return a syntax error.

Variables

Variables have been mentioned a lot in the previous chapters. Variables are storage containers of literals. They can contain data that you can use later in your program. Unlike other languages, Java is strict when it comes to variable creation. In Java, you need to declare that you want to create a variable. In the declaration, you must also state what kind of data the variable can store. For example:

int anExampleVariable;

// the previous statement says that it wants to create a variable

// with the identifier anExampleVariable

// before the identifier, there is a keyword: int

// the keyword int means that the data type that

// you want to store in the variable is an integer

anExampleVariable = 415;

// in the next statement, it assigned the integer 412 into the

// anExampleVariable variable

// to assign values to variables, you need to use the

// assignment operator (=)

// it quite similar in what you learned in Basic Algebra

int anotherExampleVariable = 55153;

// you can actually combine declaration and assignment in one statement

int a, b, c;

// you can also declare multiple variables of the same type

// just make sure that you separate them using the

// comma separator or token (,)

int d =134, e =143, f = 413;

// and you can also declare and assign multiple variables

// in one statement as well

Code Blocks

The source code is the story. Statements are the sentences. And code blocks are your paragraphs. A code block is a grouped set of statements. Statements are put inside code blocks when a programmer wants to achieve a solution or make the statements available in one call.

Code blocks are created when you create a class or method — elements in programming that you will learn in advanced books or classes. To group your statements in a code block, they must be enclosed using curly brackets or braces ({}). For example:

```
void thisIsAnExampleMethod() {

        int anExampleVariable;

        anExampleVariable = 3;

        {

                int aVariableInsideACodeBlock;

                aVariableInsideACodeBlock = 4;

        }

}
```

Scopes

In a source code, there is division of rights when it comes to variables and other elements. These rights are divided whenever a code block is created. By default, there are two divisions or scopes in a program. The first one is global. And the second one is local.

Global variables are available anywhere in your source code. On the other hand, local variables are only available on the code block where they were declared and created. In the previous example, the variable 'aVariableInsideACodeBlock' will only be useable inside the code block where it was created. If you use it outside the block, the compiler will return an error and tell you that the 'aVaraibleInsideACodeBlock' does not exist.

Also, you might have noticed that there are indentations on the source code. In Java, indentation does not matter. However, whenever you create a child code block, it is best to apply indentation to make your source code clean and readable.

Comments

Comments are the developer's best friends. Source code can become a big mess after a few hours of coding. And it is inevitable that even you will get confused with the program you wrote. To prevent that, you can place markers, reminders, labels, and explanations in comments.

Comments are handy tools. They can be put anywhere in your source code, and you do not have to worry about them affecting your program. The compiler ignores comments. As long as you provide the necessary tag or tokens, your comments will not produce any errors.

In source code editors, comments are generally highlighted in green font. But do note that in Android Studio, comments are highlighted in gray color and are italicized.

Anyway, in Java and Android, three methods of placing comments are available for you to use. You can place comments as traditional, end of line, or documentation. Below is an example of traditional.

/* to place a traditional comment, start with a forward slash then an asterisk

any following lines of text and numbers will be ignored by the compiler

you can end the traditional comment and go back to regular coding by ending

the last line of your comment with an asterisk and followed by a forward slash */

On the other hand, documentation comments have a special use in programming. Any comments you place as documentation comments will appear in certain viewers. Comments are treated as documentation comments if you place a forward slash then two asterisks /**.

To add another line of comment, place an asterisk before the line. To end a documentation comment, place an asterisk then a forward slash. For example:

/** Documentation comment example

* @writer: The One who Made this Book

*/

End of line comments are the most used comments by developers. They are handy, and are usually perfect for one line comments. To place an end of line comment, just place two forward slashes followed by your comment. You can place it in an empty line or you can place it after a physical line. The compiler will just ignore your comment. For example:

int luckyNumber = 3 //This part will be ignored

//And this part,too.

// int unluckyNumber =6 you can also use end of line comments to disable

//certain logical lines. It is much handy than deleting a possibly

//erroneous statement.

//turning a line into a comment is much better than just deleting the line

//because in case that you need the line again, you can just enable it

//by removing the two forward slashes

Expressions and Operators

Literals will be mostly useless if they are not tested, evaluated, or changed. To be capable of changing data or creating solutions, you will need to use operators and create expressions.

In Mathematics, operators are addition, subtraction, division, and multiplication. All of them, together with other operators for logic, comparison, and etcetera, are included in programming. On the other hand, expressions are combinations of operators and literals, variables, and/or functions, which can be evaluated.

Below is an example of expressions:

int x = 2 + 3;

int y = x * 2;

int z = x - y

With those statements, variable x now contains 5, variable y contains 10, and variable z now contains -5. As a tip, always make sure that you declare the variable first before you use them. Below is a bad example of an expression:

b = 1 + f;

In this example, variable b and f are not declared. When this code is compiled, the compiler will provide an error and stop. First, the variable b is not declared. Second, variable does not contain any value yet. Third, you cannot add 1 to something undefined. Fourth, what data type is variable b expecting?

Also, like Mathematics, operators follow an order of precedence. Some operators are evaluated first before any other operators. For example:

int j;

j = 2 + 5 * 3 + 4;

Variable j is equal to 21. j = 2 + 5 * 3 + 4 = 2 + 15 + 4 = 21

j = (2 + 5) * 3 + 4;

Variable j is equal to 25. j = (2 + 5) * 3 + 4 = 7 * 3 + 4 = 21 + 4 = 25

j = 2 + 5 * (3 + 4);

Variable j is equal to 37. j = 2 + 5 * (3 + 4) = 2 + 5 * 7 = 2 + 35 = 37

j = (2 + 5) * (3 + 4);

Variable j is equal to 49. j = (2 + 5) * (3 + 4) = 7 * 7 = 49

Since parentheses have the highest precedence of all, any expressions enclosed on it gets evaluated first. And due to that, the evaluation keeps changing every time the parentheses are moved. Also, when the parentheses are removed, the multiplication operator becomes the one with the highest precedence. Because of that, it will be evaluated first before the addition expression.

As of now, you will be mostly using arithmetic operators and the assignment operator (=). Once you get the hang of designing your app, then you should move into creating conditions and checks. Looping also will help. And when you learn those, you will be introduced to comparing and logical operators.

An Example

Check out this example below. It is a default Java source code for a new app in Android Studio.

package com.example.admin.myapplication;

import android.support.v7.app.ActionBarActivity;
import android.os.Bundle;
import android.view.Menu;
import android.view.MenuItem;

public class MainActivity **extends** ActionBarActivity {

@Override

```java
protected void onCreate(Bundle savedInstanceState) {
super.onCreate(savedInstanceState);
setContentView(R.layout.activity_main);
}


@Override
public boolean onCreateOptionsMenu(Menu menu) {
// Inflate the menu; this adds items to the action bar if it is
present.
getMenuInflater().inflate(R.menu.menu_main, menu);
return true;
}


@Override
public boolean onOptionsItemSelected(MenuItem item) {
// Handle action bar item clicks here. The action bar will
// automatically handle clicks on the Home/Up button, so
long
// as you specify a parent activity in AndroidManifest.xml.
int id = item.getItemId();

//noinspection SimplifiableIfStatement
if (id == R.id.action_settings) {
return true;
}

return super.onOptionsItemSelected(item);
}
}
```

Introduction to XML

Thanks to the IDEs (Android Studio and Eclipse), fiddling with XML files in your Android app will not be too necessary. Nevertheless, it is still essential that you become familiar with it. After all, most of the resources and activities in your app are written in XML files. You will need to tweak some XML files from time to time.

Also, compared to coding in Java, XML reading and writing are much easier. After all, XML is more like a different method of creating data structure. If you are familiar with HTML (the markup language used for webpages), you will find it effortless to understand XML. Below is the content of a new app's XML file for an activity or page in the app:

```
<RelativeLayout
xmlns:android="http://schemas.android.com/apk/
res/android"
 xmlns:tools="http://schemas.android.com/tools"
android:layout_width="match_parent"
 android:layout_height="match_parent"
android:paddingLeft="@dimen/activity_horizontal
_margin"

android:paddingRight="@dimen/activity_horizonta
l_margin"

android:paddingTop="@dimen/activity_vertical_m
argin"

android:paddingBottom="@dimen/activity_vertical
_margin" tools:context=".MainActivity">

 <TextView        android:text="@string/hello_world"
android:layout_width="wrap_content"
 android:layout_height="wrap_content" />

</RelativeLayout>
```

Markup and Content

Markup is the keywords, words, and syntax that organizes the XML file. On the other hand, content is the data placed in the markup. And that content will be available to the functions that will use them. Usually, the content in an Android app's XML files is used to display information on the app's activities or pages.

Elements and Tags

Just like in HTML, XML uses opening and closing tags to enclose content or nest other tags or elements. Tags are usually enclosed in less (<) and greater (>) than signs — or chevrons.

Users can set their own tags. On the other hand, depending on the machine or application that will use the XML files, the XML coder might need to write predefined tags. Of course, due to that, processing of XML files can be different from one machine and application to another. One of the predefined or used tags or elements in an Android app is TextView. Other applications or machines cannot understand that tag.

Every content or element enclosed with an opening and closing tag is a markup line. By the way, an opening tag is enclosed with chevrons. The closing tag is prefixed with a forward slash (/) and is enclosed with chevrons. For example:

<RelativeLayout>

    <...some nested content over here...>

</RelativeLayout>

In Android XMLs, markup elements with opening and closing tags can contain or nest other elements or content inside it. RelativeLayout is an element that can contain other elements because it is a ViewGroup element (will be discussed later).

On the other hand, elements such as TextView do not have closing tags. Instead, they are considered empty element tags. They do not require a closing tag. Instead, they must be closed by putting a space between the greater than sign and the element tag, and putting a forward slash before the greater than sign. For example:

<TextView />

All View elements, such as TextView, are empty element tags.

Attribute

Elements in an Android app have attributes. For example, TextView has a width attribute. To indicate an attribute of an element in an XML file you must put the attribute name inside the opening tag together with the value that you want to assign on the attribute. For example:

<TextView width="wrap_content" />

In Android Studio and Eclipse, attributes are automatically populated. Also, take note that attributes have default values in an Android app. If no changes are going to be made on a certain attribute in an element, there is no need to include it in the XML file.

Chapter 5: Android Studio — Creating a Project

You are now a bit familiar with Java and XML. You have also installed the necessary programs in order for you to program Android apps. Now, it is time to explore Android Studio. Most of your time will be spent using this program. And the more familiar you are with this IDE/SDK, the faster you will be able to create programs.

For now, try starting an app. Follow the steps below.

1. Execute the Android Studio program. A splash screen will appear. Please be patient. That splash screen might take a minute or two. If it is taking too long, close all the programs that you have. Once it is done loading, the welcome page will greet you.

2. In the welcome screen, look for the Start a New Android Project link/button.

3. A dialog box titled New Project will appear on the screen. In it, you will need to fill out a form. First, provide a name for your application. After that, create a reverse company domain for the package name of your application. For example, if you have a website named www.fakewebsite.com, then you titled your app Fake Calculator, you can use a package name like this: com.fakewebsite.fakecalculator.

4. After that, specify a location where your Android Studio will save your project, Click the Next button.

5. The next page will ask you about the Android devices that you want your app to be run on. Also, it will ask you about the Android version that you wish your program will be installed on. Take note that if you choose a higher version of Android, your app will not work or will not get installed on a device with a lower Android version. As of now, most people are on Ice Cream Sandwich (version 4.0). You need to choose that version if you plan to let a lot of people use your app.

6. Do note that other Android devices such as Glass, Wear, and TV are on higher versions of Android. Most smart and internet TVs use Android Lollipop. Wear uses Kitkat. Once you have decided on the devices and version of Android, click on the Next button.

7. Now, you will be on the activity page. This page will let you choose a design template for your application. Your choices will be: Tabbed, Settings, Navigation Drawer, Master/Detail Flow, Login, Google Play Services, Google Maps, Google AdMob Ads, full screen, blank activity with fragment, blank, and none.

   For now, it is best that you choose the blank activity. Choosing another template will get you confused on their content. And it best that you leave them for now, and explore them later.

8. After choosing blank activity, click on next or finish.

9. If ever you tried to choose another activity, you will be redirected to multiple customization pages. Provide the information that the pages will ask of you.

10. Once you are finished with the forms, the project will be populated. When Android Studio is done creating the project files for you, you will be sent back to the

welcome screen. Now, it is time to check your app. Click on the Open an existing Android Studio project link. Go to the folder where you saved your project.

11. Take note that every time you open Android Studio, your project will be opened immediately. If you want to create a new project, you will need to click on New or Close Project on the File menu to get back to the welcome screen.

Chapter 6: Your First Project

The app that Android Studio, or Gradle to be precise, generated for you is already a working app. The app already has the necessary files and settings, so you do not need to build your app from scratch. You can even test it on your Android emulator or device. Try it.

Test Device and Emulator Setup

The only thing that you need to setup in your Android Studio right now is the test devices and emulator. To do that, fiddle with the debugging and run options of the IDE. Click on the Run button on the Menu bar. After that, choose Edit Configurations on the context menu. The Run/Debug Configurations dialog box will appear.

Click on the Defaults option on the leftmost part of the window. Then click on Android Application. In this new page, you can choose where you want to perform a test run of your Android app. You can choose the Android emulator or your Android device.

If you choose the Android emulator, you will need to set it up. First, you will need to choose the device and version that you want to emulate in your computer. Again, running the emulator can be a pain because it is slow.

On the other hand, if you choose a device, connect your Android smartphone or tablet on your computer. Let the computer identify it. Once your computer finishing connecting with the Android the device, your device's name will appear on the list. Take note, you will need to turn on the developer options on your Android.

Whenever you run or debug your program, Android Studio will compile, send, install, and run it on your device — the same goes if you choose the emulator. To test run your app, choose an activity on your project. The run button should be clickable after that. Once you click on run, wait for your device or emulator to open your app.

SDK Update

After you have installed your SDK and Android Studio, you might already have run the SDK manager and updated your repositories. However, it is best that you repeat it again. In case that you have chosen an Android version that did not come in the previous update, then you will need to update manually.

To open the SDK manager, click Tools > Android > SDK manager. To update, make sure that the Updates/New box is ticked. On your right, you will see the Install packages button. Click it.

If ever the repositories that you will download come with licenses, another window will appear. You will need to agree on the terms imposed on those licenses. Also, remember that the updates are usually big files. You might need to wait a while before the manager finishes updating your Android Studio.

Getting Familiar with the IDE

If this is your first time experiencing using an IDE, you may be overwhelmed right now. After all, a bunch of buttons, links, and windows are in front of you, and you have no idea about their functions. If you have experienced using Eclipse, the interface of Android Studio is somewhat similar to it.

The Toolbar

If you need to access tools for your app, such as debugging, editing commands, and file management, just look for the toolbar. It should below the Menu bar by default.

The Tool Buttons

On the bottom, left, and right sides of the IDE, Tool Buttons are scattered. The Tool Buttons bring up important tool dialog boxes and widgets. A few of those tool windows are build variants, Gradle, Maven projects, to do, messages, android, captures, structure, favorites, and project.

The Project Tool Window

This window lets you explore all the files in your project. You can open the files directly from the Project window. Take note that all of the important files of your project or app are under the app folder. In case you want to edit the XML files of your activities, you can just go to app -> src -> main -> res -> layout.

The Status Bar

Just like any regular status bar, the status bar of Android Studio will provide you with some snippets of information.

The Navigation Bar

Aside from the Project Tool window, you can explore your files using the navigation bar. The navigation bar is like an address bar in your computer browser.

The Tab Bar

Just a few pixels below the navigation bar, the tab bar can be found. If you have multiple files opened, you can take advantage of the tab bar to prevent the hassle of digging for the files you need to edit.

The Workspace

In the center of the IDE is the workspace. Editing, developing, and designing your app will happen here. The window that will be opened in the workspace depends on what type of file that you are editing. For example, in the case that you are going to edit a Java file, Android Studio's source code will be in the workspace. On the other hand, opening a picture will make Android Studio open its own image viewer.

In the case that you open an XML file under the layouts directory, you will be provided with two editing modes. The first one is Text or the source code editor. The second one is the Design or the Live Preview mode. You can change modes by clicking the designated button for each mode in the bottom of the workspace.

The Palette

When you are in Design mode, the palette window will appear on the workspace. It will contain the elements that you can insert in your app's graphical user interface or activities. You can just click on an element, drag it, and drop it on the workspace's live preview of your application. They are categorized into eight types: Expert, Layouts, Text Fields, Widgets, Date and Time, Containers, and Custom.

The Component Tree

The component tree gives you a directory list of all the elements in the activity that is opened. It will give you an idea of what elements are included in the activity. And which ViewGroups your View elements are in.

When you click on an element in the component tree, that element will be highlighted on the layout view window and all its attributes will be listed on the properties window.

The Layout View Window

During your early days in developing Android apps, you will be most likely play around in the layout view area. It contains the interactive live window. On it, you can just drag and drop elements that you want to appear in the activities or pages of your app.

It provides an accurate view of how your app will look like on the device that you want to run your program. You can even zoom in and zoom out the preview of your app. Also, you can view your app in landscape or portrait mode and see your app on a smartphone or tablet. If you want, you can check the preview of your app in Android TV or Wear.

Take note that every time that you do something in the layout view window, Android Studio will generate the correct code for the design that you want. By the way, in case that your computer does not have high specs, expect that moving elements around the live preview will be slow.

The Properties Window

With the properties window, you can spare yourself of looking at reference pages just to remember a certain attribute. Any changes that you make in the properties window will automatically reflect in the code.

XML and Source Code Editor

When switching to Text mode or source code editor, the properties window, component tree, and palette will not be visible.

The live preview will still be seen while the source code editor is on the workspace. However, you will not be able to drag and drop any elements on it. In case that you double click on something in the live preview, the workspace will be reverted back to Design view.

The source code editor has the most basic features. It has syntax highlighting, advanced keyword completion, and code folding.

Chapter 7: Editing the Default App

The default app that Android Studio created does nothing except from showing a TextView element in the main activity page, which says Hello World. In this part of the book, you will be taught some basic editing of the app.

First of all, you should know the difference between a View and Viewgroup element. View elements are commonly called widgets. A few of those widgets are sliders, buttons, and etcetera.

Unlike View elements, Viewgroups are invisible containers for View elements. They define how the View elements will be laid out on the screen. They also serve as a grouping mechanism of elements in your activities. It makes it easier to manage the elements in your apps with them around. If you are knowledgeable about HTML, Viewgroups are like div elements.

By the way, you can also include another Viewgroup element inside a Viewgroup. However, take note that View elements will never have any element inside them. View elements will never be parent elements. They will be stuck as child objects.

Go and check your project's component tree. As you can see, under Device Screen, you will see two other items. The first one is RelativeLayout. The second one is TextView. The RelativeLayout is a Viewgroup. And inside that Viewgroup is TextView, which is a View object.

When dragging elements in your app's live preview, you might have noticed that some green lines and arrows appearing on the edges of your elements. They are guiding lines. And they makes it easier for you to place your elements in position in relation with the other elements. In advanced subjects, take note that the placement of elements may change if the Viewgroup layout is changed.

For example, RelativeLayout enforces relative positioning of the elements inside it. If you change the Viewgroup to another Layout element, the positioning stored in the XML file may confuse the live preview and the compiler. So, do not just replace the tags in the XML. If you want to do that, you should check Android Viewgroups and layout references. Know how they work first.

Try adding more widgets or elements in your app. Try changing the attributes of the elements, and see what happens. Also, always check the changes that happen in the XML file of your activities. If you are satisfied with the design of your app, try running it on your device and see how it works!

Conclusion

Thank you again for downloading this book!

I hope this book was able to help you learn more about Android programming, and inspired you create your very own Android app!

The next step is to begin and practice what you have read about. Learning is one thing, but actually doing is another. Being proficient with Android App Development will take some practice, but is definitely worth it! Good luck!

Finally, if you enjoyed this book, please take the time to share your thoughts and post a review on Amazon. It'd be greatly appreciated!

Thank you and good luck!